THE COURTIN'

BY

JAMES RUSSELL LOWELL

ILLUSTRATED BY WINSLOW HOMER

PUBLISHED BY
WALKER AND COMPANY, NEW YORK
IN ASSOCIATION WITH
THE DEPARTMENT OF PRINTING AND GRAPHIC ARTS
HARVARD COLLEGE LIBRARY
1968

This volume is an exact facsimile
of the 1874 edition of *The Courtin'*
with illustrations by Winslow Homer.
It was initially published in Boston
by James R. Osgood and Company.

This edition is limited to 3,000 copies

Library of Congress Catalog Card Number: 68-16800

The COURTIN'

BY

JAMES RUSSELL LOWELL

Illustrated By

WINSLOW HOMER

THE COURTIN'

BY

JAMES RUSSELL LOWELL

ILLUSTRATED BY WINSLOW HOMER

BOSTON

JAMES R. OSGOOD AND COMPANY

Late Ticknor & Fields, and Fields, Osgood, & Co.

1874

CAMBRIDGE. MASS.

LIST OF ILLUSTRATIONS.

REPRODUCED IN HELIOTYPE FROM DRAWINGS BY WINSLOW HOMER.

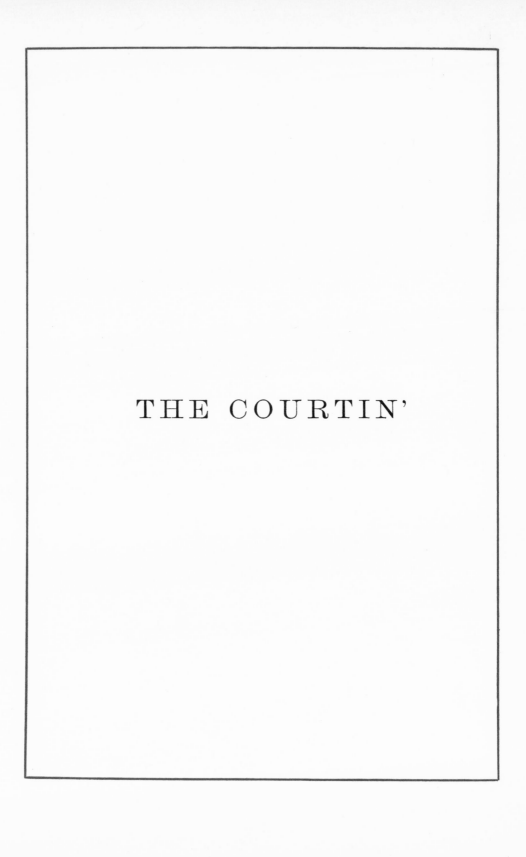

THE COURTIN'

"Zekle crep' up quite unbeknown
An' peeked in thru' the winder."

THE COURTIN'.

GOD makes sech nights, all white an' still
  Fur 'z you can look or listen,
Moonshine an' snow on field an' hill,
  All silence an' all glisten.

Zekle crep' up quite unbeknown
  An' peeked in thru' the winder,
An' there sot Huldy all alone,
  'Ith no one nigh to hender.

A fireplace filled the room's one side
  With half a cord o' wood in —
There warn't no stoves (tell comfort died)
  To bake ye to a puddin'.

"There sot Huldy all alone,
'Ith no one nigh to hender."

THE COURTIN'.

The wa'nut logs shot sparkles out
　　Towards the pootiest, bless her,
An' leetle flames danced all about
　　The chiny on the dresser.

Agin the chimbley crook-necks hung,
　　An' in amongst 'em rusted
The ole queen's-arm thet gran'ther Young
　　Fetched back from Concord busted.

The very room, coz she was in,
　　Seemed warm from floor to ceilin',
An' she looked full ez rosy agin
　　Ez the apples she was peelin'.

'T was kin' o' kingdom-come to look
　　On sech a blessed cretur,
A dogrose blushin' to a brook
　　Ain't modester nor sweeter.

"You want to see my Pa, I s'pose?"

THE COURTIN'.

He was six foot o' man, A 1,
    Clean grit an' human natur';
None could n't quicker pitch a ton
    Nor dror a furrer straighter.

He 'd sparked it with full twenty gals,
    Hed squired 'em, danced 'em, druv 'em,
Fust this one, an' then thet, by spells —
    All is, he could n't love 'em.

But long o' her his veins 'ould run
    All crinkly like curled maple,
The side she breshed felt full o' sun
    Ez a south slope in Ap'il.

She thought no v'ice hed sech a swing
    Ez hisn in the choir;
My! when he made Ole Hunderd ring,
    She *knowed* the Lord was nigher.

"Says he, 'I'd better call agin.'"

THE COURTIN'.

An' she 'd blush scarlit, right in prayer,
   When her new meetin'-bunnet
Felt somehow thru' its crown a pair
   O' blue eyes sot upon it.

Thet night, I tell ye, she looked *some!*
   She seemed to 've gut a new soul,
For she felt sartin-sure he 'd come,
   Down to her very shoe-sole.

She heered a foot, an' knowed it tu,
   A-raspin' on the scraper, —
All ways to once her feelins flew
   Like sparks in burnt-up paper.

He kin' o' l'itered on the mat,
   Some doubtfle o' the sekle,
His heart kep' goin' pity-pat,
   But hern went pity Zekle.

" An' . . . . Wal, he up an' kist her."

An' yit she gin her cheer a jerk
 Ez though she wished him furder,
An' on her apples kep' to work,
 Parin' away like murder.

" You want to see my Pa, I s'pose ? "
 " Wal . . . . no . . . . I come dasignin' " —
" To see my Ma ? She 's sprinklin' clo'es
 Agin to-morrer's i'nin'."

To say why gals acts so or so,
 Or don't, 'ould be presumin' ;
Mebby to mean *yes* an' say *no*
 Comes nateral to women.

He stood a spell on one foot fust,
 Then stood a spell on t'other,
An' on which one he felt the wust
 He could n't ha' told ye nuther.

" An' teary roun' the lashes."

THE COURTIN'.

Says he, "I'd better call agin";
　Says she, "Think likely, Mister";
Thet last word pricked him like a pin,
　An' . . . . Wal, he up an' kist her.

When Ma bimeby upon 'em slips,
　Huldy sot pale ez ashes,
All kin' o' smily roun' the lips
　An' teary roun' the lashes.

For she was jes' the quiet kind
　Whose naturs never vary,
Like streams that keep a summer mind
　Snowhid in Jenooary.

The blood clost roun' her heart felt glued
　Too tight for all expressin',
Tell mother see how metters stood,
　And gin 'em both her blessin'.

" In meetin' come nex' Sunday."

Then her red come back like the tide
    Down to the Bay o' Fundy,
An' all I know is they was cried
    In meetin' come nex' Sunday.